The World of Nature

INSECTS

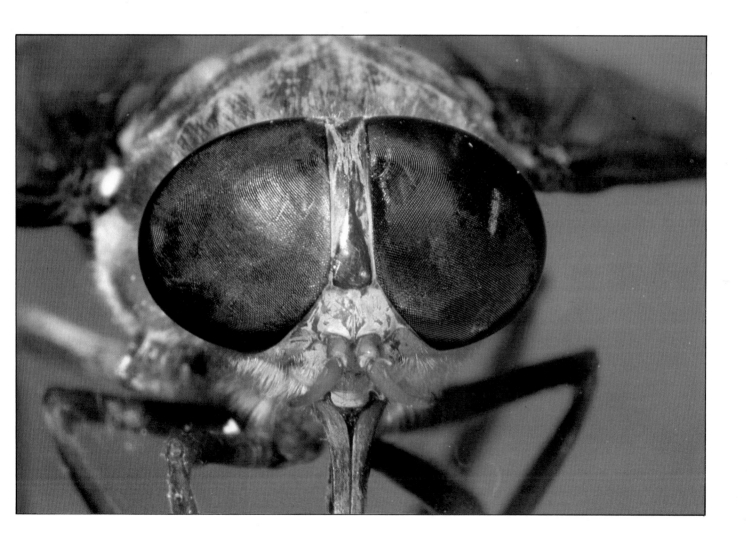

GALLERY BOOKS

An Imprint of W. H. Smith Publishers Inc.
112 Madison Avenue
New York City 10016

This edition first published in U.S.
in 1991 by Gallery Books,
an imprint of W.H. Smith Publishers, Inc.
112 Madison Avenue, New York, New York 10016

ISBN 0-8317-9568-9

Printed and bound in Spain

For rights information about the photographs in
this book please contact:

The Image Bank
111 Fifth Avenue, New York, NY 10003

Producer: Solomon M. Skolnick
Writer: Marcus Schneck
Design Concept: Lesley Ehlers
Designer: Ann-Louise Lipman
Editor: Joan E. Ratajack
Production: Valerie Zars
Photo Researcher: Edward Douglas
Assistant Photo Researcher: Robert V. Hale
Editorial Assistant: Carol Raguso

Title page: **No matter how common they may be, insects have an otherworldly appearance that some people find difficult to appreciate. This is a close-up of a common horsefly.** *Opposite:* **Ladybird beetles, which are among the most beneficial insects to have around the garden, gather in large clusters amid leaf litter to hibernate for the winter.**

Insect: 1. Any of the small invertebrate animals belonging to the class *Insecta*. **2.** Someone who is small and contemptible.

Bug: 1. Any of various wingless or four-winged insects. **2.** To annoy or pester.

These definitions reflect the low regard that humans generally hold for the insect world. The same terms used to describe those small fellow creatures have also come to refer to undesirable traits in people.

The antibug industry – those myriad companies that produce insecticides, repellents, bug zappers, fly swatters, screened enclosures, and other products – rakes in hundreds of millions of dollars each year because of humanity's dislike of "creepy crawlies." Most people would be hard pressed to survey their households without locating at least one antibug device or concoction.

The mere sight of a cockroach scooting across the kitchen floor or of wasps building their nest in the eaves of the house or of an earwig hiding among the tight leaves of a cabbage head can repulse people who believe immediate action must be taken against these insect invaders.

Although it's true that few of us can help but marvel over a mud-puddle gathering of tiger swallowtail butterflies *(Papilio glaucus)*, the number of empathy-inspiring insects

The long-jawed longhorn beetle is an adversary of the lumber industry because of its larvae's penchant for tunneling into cut logs that are lying on the forest floor. *Left:* More than 20,000 species of longhorn beetles have been identified worldwide, most in tropical regions such as Costa Rica, where this iridescent specimen thrives.

The primary defense of a blister beetle lies in a chemical known as cantharidin, which the insect emits when threatened. Cantharidin causes blisters on human skin. *Below:* The spotted cucumber beetle's larva is often referred to as the corn rootworm, a name that attests to its status as an agricultural pest. *Overleaf:* Hercules beetles are among the largest insects on earth, measuring as much as two-and-a-half inches in length. The male of the species sports horns, but the female has none.

seems limited. Humans tend to extend their contempt for the relatively few harmful insects to the harmless ones as well. We curse the cabbage white butterfly *(Pieris rapae)* for the damage done to crops by its small, blue-green caterpillar. And we draw back from the massive pincers of the elephant stag beetle *Lucanus elephus),* although it's actually as harmless as the swallowtail butterfly.

Much of this disdain can be traced back to those insects that are truly harmful to people, their animals, or their food.

Malaria and yellow fever, caused by protozoans transmitted through the bite of any of 60 different mosquito species of the genus Anopheles, still strike an estimated 100 million people in tropical regions each year and is fatal in about one percent of the cases.

Bubonic plague, or the Black Death, which wiped out almost half the population of Europe during the Middle Ages, was spread by the bites of fleas *(Xenopsylla cheopis)* carried on rats that infested human habitations of the day. Fleas are still a major concern for pet owners today, not because of plague, but for other diseases they may spread.

Beyond direct health threats, insects are linked with billions of dollars worth of lost and damaged

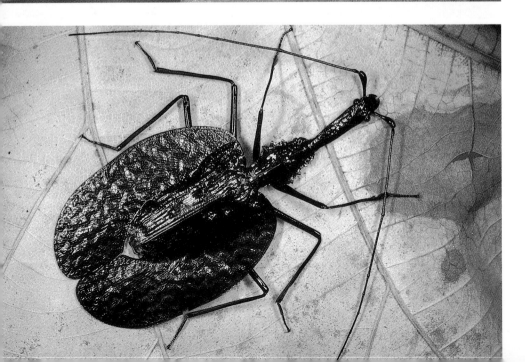

Top to bottom: **Ten-lined June beetles cruise over fields and congregate at lights on warm summer evenings. The glorious beetle, which just might be the most beautiful of all North American beetles, is an endangered species and should not be added to collections. The ghost walker beetle from Sumatra features one of the most unusual body configurations in the insect world; the exact reasons for the gigantic, rounded abdomen are not fully understood.** *Opposite:* **A predatory beetle jabs its spearlike proboscis into its prey to suck the body juices from the victim.**

The Arizona blister beetle is one of the lesser-known members of the family *Meloidae*. Some phases of its life cycle have yet to be identified. *Below:* The harlequin longhorn beetle leads a secretive, nocturnal existence, remaining in hiding during daylight hours. *Opposite:* Scarab beetles are generally dung scavengers. When one of these insects locates some dung, it bites off a piece and rolls it into a ball larger than itself. The beetle rolls the ball along the ground until it finds an appropriate spot to bury the dung and itself. It can then eat the dung in the underground chamber in relative safety.

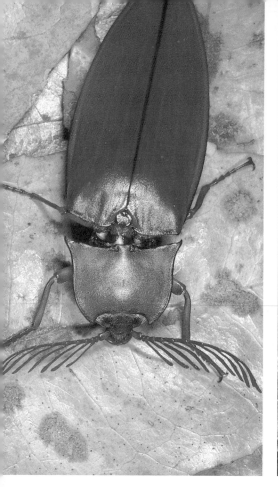

Top, left to right: Click beetles were named for the sound they make when flipping themselves out of an overturned position and into to the air to right themselves. The tortoise beetle is named for its "shell" (composed of wing covers and a shield rather than a one-piece carapace), which has an appearance similar to that of its reptilian namesake. This adult tiger beetle is a fierce predator on nearly all smaller creatures. *Below:* The huge, antlerlike jaws of the male stag beetle give this family of insects its common name. These beetles can be tenacious in defending themselves. *Opposite:* The black-spot tortoise beetle is one member of the *Cassidinae* family, which has representatives in the warmer regions of the world.

food each year. The insects responsible for this loss – which is estimated to be as high as 30 to 50 percent of all edible food in some regions – have earned the entire group a bad reputation.

The previously mentioned caterpillar of the cabbage white butterfly, also called the European cabbage butterfly, eats its way through countless fields of cabbage and related crucifers annually. Mistakenly released near Montreal in the 1860's, this species has become one of the continent's most abundant and successful butterflies, to the dismay of the agricultural community.

Another non-native, introduced species – the gypsy moth *(Porthetria dispar)* – has had a similarly devastating impact on the hardwood forests of eastern North America. Millions of acres of trees have been stripped of their leaves by the hairy caterpillars. Also like the cabbage white, the gypsy moth was not a resident of North America until the 1860's when it was accidentally introduced in Massachusetts from Europe.

Livestock has not escaped the insect attack. The larvae of screwworm flies *(Callitroga hominivorax)* have been known to decimate whole cattle and sheep herds. The larvae of heel flies *(Hypoderma lineata)* have cost cattle ranchers hundreds of millions of dollars in injured and killed animals.

Top to bottom: **The long beak of the female acorn weevil allows it to bore an opening into the nut, where the insect then deposits its eggs. An accidental import from Mexico, the boll weevil has devastated cotton crops in parts of the southern U.S. ever since its introduction in the 1800's. The aptly named ferocious water bug seizes its prey in its powerful forelegs, jabs its beak into the victim, and sucks out the body juices.**

Above: The giant weevil (left), at a maximum length of about three inches, is a Goliath among the 40,000-plus species of weevils that have been identified. Most are only about an eighth of an inch long. Periodical cicadas (left) emerge from underground after 13 or 17 years (depending on where they live), the time it takes for nymphs to complete their growth. The nymph then attaches itself to the nearest tree, sheds its shell, and begins its few-weeks-long adult life. *Below:* The order *Coleoptera,* which includes species such as this red-striped weevil, is the most numerous animal order on earth.

This page and opposite: An adult grand western cicada emerges from the dried skin of its nymph form. It then rests on the stiff shell of its former self while its new exterior hardens. The adult, which eats nothing at all, focuses entirely on its mission of creating the next generation.

But all this damage is the work of only a small minority of the insect world. Some estimates place the proportion of truly harmful insects at only one percent. Apart from the few exceptions and despite misconceptions and biases, nearly all species of insects, therefore, can be classified as harmless to humans.

Many species must even be considered beneficial. Several thousand plant species, including more than 60 of the domestic varieties grown commercially in the U.S., rely on insects for pollination. Some insects also prey upon other, more harmful, insects. For example, the familiar ladybug of the Coccinellidae family feasts upon thousands of destructive aphids each summer. Still other beetles act to replenish the richness of earth's soil by scavenging and breaking down dead plant and animal matter. The various carrion and scarab beetles make their contributions in this way.

There are also those insects that directly provide usable products. Millions of pounds of honey are consumed each year in the U.S. alone, both as pure honey and as a sweetening ingredient in other products. Several million pounds of beeswax are used every year in the U.S., not only in candles, but in lubricants, ointments, polishes, and varnishes as well.

Preceding page: When stinkbugs such as this Malaysian species are disturbed, they spray relatively large amounts of foul-smelling liquid to discourage potential attackers. *This page, top to bottom:* The pronotum of this treehopper extends out over the insect's back, giving it the highly successful camouflage of appearing to be a thorn on the side of a plant. Most species of leafhoppers, of which there are 2,500 in North America alone, emit a sweet liquid that attracts ants, flies, and other small insects. When feeding, the scarlet and green leafhopper injects saliva that blocks the normal flow of sap through the plant and causes it to wither.

Although synthetic fibers have captured a large share of the market, real silk is still produced only by the silkworm *(Bombyx mori)* and several related species. New chemical compounds have made inroads into the commercial dye industry, but the ground-up bodies of many scale insects of the family Coccidae are still used.

Beyond all human concerns over the commercial benefits of, or losses to, insects, these small creatures play an essential role in the broad scheme of life on earth. Existing near the lower end of the food chain, insects provide food for nearly all of the more noticeable animal life on the planet.

Birds, bats, lizards, frogs, snakes, turtles, fish, moles, ant-eaters, and the like all prey upon insects. But much larger, and often less expected, animals include sizable amounts of insects in their diets. The massive black bear eats thousands upon thousands of beetles, ants, bees, and their larvae each year. Even the stealthy mountain lion is not above making a meal of a field full of grasshoppers.

As would be expected of a class of animals preyed on by so many others, insects are incredibly numerous and diverse. There are more insects, and more types of insects, on earth than there are of all other animal life that can be seen without a microscope. The ant species alone accounts for between 10 and 15 percent of the total weight of all land-based animal life.

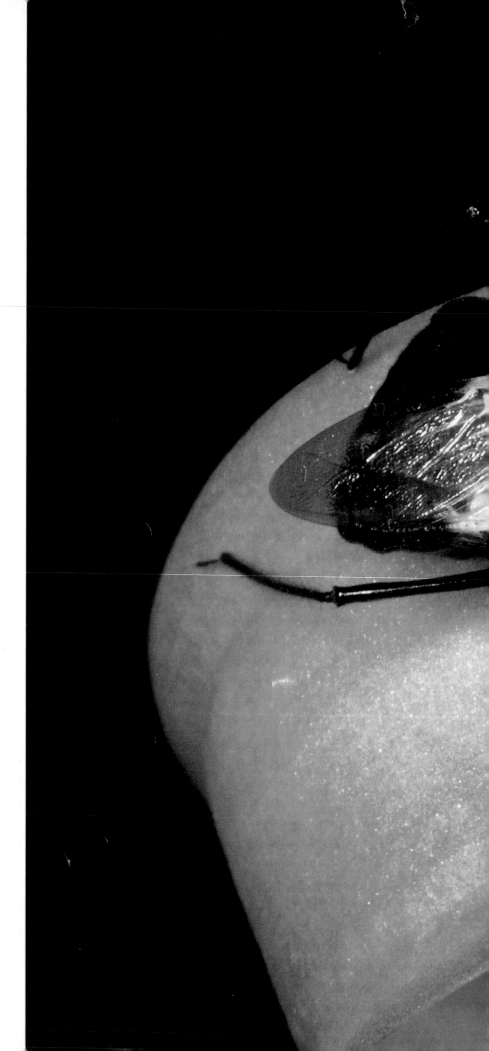

The assassin bug attacks its prey by stabbing with its long, sharp proboscis and injecting venom. The same tube is then used to suck the body juices from the victim. *Overleaf:* **Nymphs of the squash bug begin to hatch from a cluster of eggs that an adult female laid on the underside of a squash leaf. The feeding nymphs will soon cause the leaves to blacken and dry.**

Above: When isolated in a photograph, this late nymph (left) of an orchid mantis is strikingly obvious. However, since the insect spends most of its life among the flowers for which it is named, it is very well camouflaged. The neck (right) of most mantid species is flexible enough to permit the insect to look over its shoulder. This feat cannot be matched by the insects of any other family. *Below:* The familiar praying mantis of eastern North America is much smaller than most people assume—the insect measures just two-and-one-half inches long when fully grown. *Opposite:* Safely hidden beneath the leaflike camouflage of its outstretched wings, a leaf-imitating mantis eats the katydid it snared. *Overleaf:* The dead-leaf mantis is practically indistinguishable from the leaf litter on the Malaysian rain forest floor, where it waits motionless for its prey to happen along.

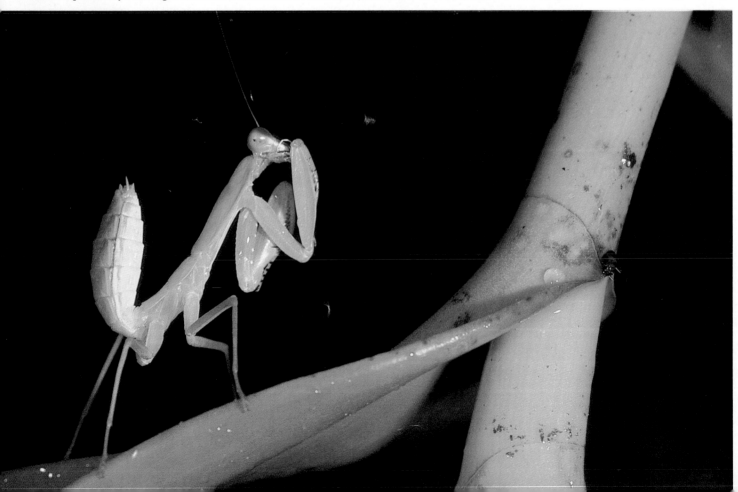

More than a million different species in 29 different orders within the class Insecta have been described and cataloged to date, but some observers estimate that number to be as little as five percent of the actual number of insect species that exist. There are many species that will never be known. With the destruction of crucial habitats, such as rain forests, they will become extinct before researchers ever come into contact with them.

The vast array of insects occurs virtually everywhere on the planet. Even icebound Antarctica is not without its own hardy races of fleas and mites. Every type of water, from fresh to brackish to salt and everything in between, harbors some insect species. Every land form, from barren desert to concrete-covered metropolis, is their host.

Approximately 100,000 species have been recorded in North America. Even New York City has many diverse insect residents – 15,000 different species according to one count.

Despite such variety, most insects share several characteristics. They have three major divisions to their bodies: head, thorax, and abdomen. The head usually has two

Preceding page: If a small insect lands on this seemingly safe branch of leaves, chances are it will be snared in the clawed front legs of this well-concealed female moving leaf mantis. *Opposite:* The twiglike walkingstick is hidden from predatory birds. But if a bird does attack and the walkingstick loses a leg in the ensuing fray, it has the incredible ability to regenerate that leg. *This page, above:* The spur-throated grasshopper of the south central U.S. is a member of the family of short-horned grasshoppers, which are relatives of the "locusts" whose plagues are described in the Bible. *Right:* When this tropical grasshopper flits away from danger, the colorful undersides of its wings alternate with the dull, gray-brown tops, and confuse the predator.

Above: Insects have developed an incredible array of camouflage devices to avoid their enemies. Mimicking the leaves of plants (left) where they spend a great deal of time is one such ruse. An immature short-horned grasshopper (right) is dwarfed by the flower petals among which it rests. It is not seeking nectar, however, because grasshoppers eat leaves. *Below:* Male grasshoppers "sing" during the day by rubbing their hind legs against their front wings. They also make a clicking noise with their wings when they take off.

sets of jaws, one pair of antennae, and a pair of simple or compound eyes. Three pairs of legs and two pairs of wings are generally attached to the thorax.

The skeleton is found on the outside of the body and is therefore known as an exoskeleton. It is made of a hard substance called *chitin*, which is more flexible than bone. However, the chitin cannot grow or stretch appreciably, requiring the insect to shed its "shell" every time it grows.

Some insects hatch from their eggs as miniature replicas of their later adult forms. Others pass through several distinct phases: egg, larva, pupa, and adult. The larva is the active feeding stage, of which the butterfly's caterpillar is a prime example. The pupa is the inactive resting stage, evidenced in the butterfly's cocoon. Relatively few groups of insects give birth to live offspring rather than laying eggs.

To survive in such numbers and in such a variety of habitats, this varied class of animals has naturally acquired a wide array of physical characteristics.

Size is one such adaptation. Although all insects could be described as small in comparison to most other familiar animal life, the insect realm does indeed have its giants and its dwarfs.

Katydids, like this conehead, earn their name through their call, which sounds something like "katy-did-katy-didn't." *Right:* Most katydids spend nearly all of their lives in trees and shrubs, the leaves of which they eat. They lay their eggs inside plant stems.

The largest insects alive today are the stick insects of Indonesia of the family Phasmidae, which measure as much as 13 inches in length, and the Atlas moth *(Attacus atlas)* of India, which has a wingspan of 12 inches. Neither come close to the now-extinct dragonfly species that once buzzed about on wings that reached 24 inches from tip to tip.

At the other end of the spectrum are the tiny parasitic fairy flies of the family Mymaridae. These measure less than one-hundredth of an inch in length.

The various colors of different insects have generally evolved to help the insect survive. Many species of grasshopper, for example, match the color of their environment so closely that they are almost invisible when sitting still.

Conversely, the monarch butterfly *(Danaus plexippus)* sports a bright orange and black pair of wings that makes it stand out in almost any situation. The milkweed plants on which the monarch caterpillar feeds make the insect poisonous to predators such as birds. Thus, the butterfly's bright and easily identifiable coloring is a warning to would-be predators. Several other butterfly species, such as the viceroy *(Limenitis archippus)*, mimic the coloring of the monarch and thus gain a measure of protection from the latter's reputation.

Preceding page: The bulky body of this giant Malaysian bushcricket belies its close relationship to the slender walkingstick. *This page, top to bottom:* The courtship song of the male field cricket is a lengthy, nonstop trill that is near the uppermost range of human hearing. A continuous chirping in the basement is usually the first sign that a house cricket has taken up residence. The various camel cricket species are notable for the arch in their backs and for the fact that most males of these species do not chirp.

The coloration of still other insects is a response to their habitat. Many arctic and alpine species are very dark in color, which aids them in absorbing the limited heat offered by the sun in their northern environment.

Another critical adaptation among all insect species lies in their mouthparts. Most insects are specialized in the types of foods on which they subsist, and their mouthparts generally reflect this specialization. The grasshopper has mouthparts designed for biting and chewing. Many weevils have the long, straight proboscis needed to pierce vegetation and suck the juices from it. Mosquitoes have similar piercing and sucking mouths, but with adaptations for feeding upon animals. Adult butterflies and moths generally have a long coiled tube for a proboscis, which is unfurled to take nectar and other liquids.

The red skimmer is a dragonfly species primarily of the southern U.S. After mating in flight, the male defends the couple's territory while the female deposits her eggs in the water.
Below: Dragonflies are generally thought of as creatures of swampy, damp places. Although they do frequent such locations, the insects are strong fliers and can be seen far from water.

Above, left to right: Hatches of mayflies, often thousands of the insects at a time, can be found "coming off" streams and lakes across the globe, wherever the water is clean enough. After emerging from its nymph form, the adult mayfly generally has only a few hours to live, although some survive for several days. Damselflies, which are often misidentified as dragonflies, have much longer abdomens than their similar cousins. *Below:* Like dragonflies, the damselflies capture their prey – smaller insects – on the wing. They hold their legs in a cradlelike arrangement below the body to scoop up hapless victims.

The black flowerfly spends a great deal of its time flitting about areas with abundant flowers, a behavior similar to that of a butterfly. *Below:* Because of the housefly's well-deserved reputation as a vector of a wide variety of human diseases, it is rightly regarded as the most threatening of all insects. *Opposite:* About 4,000 facets, each of which transmits a separate image, make up each bulbous, compound eye of the housefly.

Legs, likewise, tell a great deal about the life-style of a particular insect species. Diving beetles have heavily haired legs that aid in swimming. The hind legs of worker honeybees *(Apis mellifera)* include one pollen-carrying sack each. The hind legs of the grasshopper are muscular and taut like springs, allowing the insect to jump great distances as a means of escape. The spadelike front legs of mole crickets reveal that they spend much of their lives tunneling through the soil. The front legs of the dragonfly are long and thin, and covered with stiff bristles. They are cradled into a basket of sorts below the insect, allowing it to scoop its prey from the air as it flies.

Along with this diversity of physical characteristics, the insect world has also evolved a bewildering array of behavioral survival techniques. The social life-style of the honeybee is perhaps the best known of these strange adaptations. The entire life of the hive is centered on the queen, the source of all new life. She is maintained at all costs by the worker bees and is fed a rich diet of royal jelly for her entire life, which might extend as long as five years. The eggs she lays will produce a colony of as many as 80,000 worker bees.

Preceding page: Huge termite hills are common to the drier grassland regions of the world, such as the interior of Australia and Africa. The structure and strength of the hill is similar to that of a rock, although it was built by the insects one tiny speck at a time. *This page, top to bottom:* A homeowner's worst nightmare, termites attack all types of wood by chewing tunnels with the grain of the wood until the wood collapses. A fire ant bite tends to feel like a burn, which gave rise to the insect's common name. The giant forest ant of Malaysia is one of many species of honeypot ants, certain members of which spend their entire lives in the nest serving as living honeypots; they are fed nectar by other ants and store it until it is needed by other members of the colony.

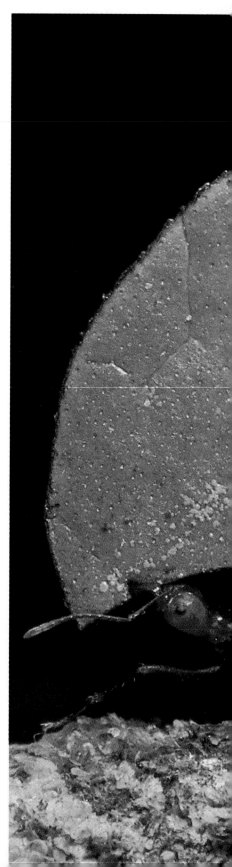

Weaver ants pull leaves together into tight bundles to form the nest for their queen, eggs, and larvae. *Below:* Leaf-cutter ants carry seemingly impossible chunks of leaves back to their nests, where the plant matter is turned into compost used to nurture the bed of fungus that the colony grows as food.

Each spring or early summer, a few of the eggs will produce new queens. At this point the old queen, accompanied by a swarm of workers, leaves to begin a new colony. The first of the new queens to emerge will kill all the others and become the focus of the hive.

Throughout this process the workers toil endlessly with the constant work of the hive and colony. It is their responsibility to gather, store, and feed honey to the larvae and the queen. Like all functions of the hive, this is a group activity. When a worker finds a particularly bountiful patch of flowers, she returns to the hive and tells her sister workers about it through a "dance." Built into her movements are the distance and direction of the nectar source.

The workers also must build, maintain, and protect the hive. Encroaching enemies are stung without hesitation, even though the sting means certain death for the bee. The stinger rips from the bee's abdomen and remains in the victim, and without that stinger the bee soon dies. In their constant vigil, they use the movements of their bodies and wings to maintain a constant temperature inside the hive that is healthiest for the developing larvae.

A third group of colony members, the male drones, live only to mate with the queen. Once they have performed that duty, they are permitted no more food and soon die.

Top to bottom: **A female thread-waisted wasp stings a tent caterpillar to immobilize it; the living caterpillar will be a host and a food source to the wasp's eggs. Unlike bees, which can sting only once, a female yellow jacket will sting a perceived attacker again and again at the slightest provocation. These wasps, a nocturnal species of the *Polybiin* family, construct nests with one open end that they guard with their own bodies.** *Opposite:* **Paper wasps are named for the hanging, paperlike nests that teams of females construct in the spring. Like paper, the nest material is made of wood pulp and water, the result of chewing by the insect.**

As a bumblebee buzzes from one flower to another, it carries pollen with it, performing the cross-pollination that the plants need to produce their next generation. *Below:* A honeybee hive constantly hums with activity, as the bees go about the endless duties required to maintain their society and the species. *Opposite:* Although the development of new, self-pollinating species of agricultural plants has lessened their importance, honeybees continue to be the most agriculturally valuable insect.

People began the domestic breeding and raising of the silkworm moth more than 4,000 years ago to benefit from the silk-making abilities of the species' caterpillar. *Below:* The caterpillar of the silk moth feeds almost exclusively on the leaves of the mulberry, one of the facts that helped to limit human use of the insect to the Far East for nearly 2,000 years.

The gypsy moth was introduced into the U.S. by an entrepreneur who hoped to create a silk industry based on the insect. Unfortunately, the insect became a devastating forest pest throughout the eastern part of the country. *Below:* The caterpillars of most tent caterpillar species are highly social, living together by the hundreds in silk tents spun in protected locations.

Although they produce no honeylike substances of their own, several species of ants – including the common red ant (*Formica* spp.) – gather, maintain, and milk herds of aphids for the honeydew that they produce. Some species, such as the Texas shed-builder ant *(Cremastogaster lineolata),* actually construct shieldlike structures of chewed vegetable matter over their herds.

Unlike the bee, most ants cannot store the honeydew for future use. But within a few ant species, living storage containers for the sweet elixir have evolved. These enlarged ants are generally unable to move around and tend to remain in the nest, where they are fed from aphids brought to them and where they in turn give up some of their stored honeydew to other members of the nest.

Some South American species of ants take an even more active role in raising their "livestock." These tiny agriculturalists cut circular bits of vegetation, which they then carry back into the nest. There they add the vegetation to a growing heap of compost, upon which grows the fungus that the ants cultivate and eat. Several species of ambrosia beetles of the family Scolytidae perform the same feat, growing their fungi in the wood chips of their nest inside a tree.

Preceding page: **The polyphemus moth was named after one of the Cyclops of Greek mythology for the huge eyespot that is more visible on the upper side of its wings. It is a resident of the deciduous forests of North America.** *This page, top to bottom:* **Like many species of moth and butterfly, the emperor moth is sexually dimorphic, which means the male, like this gaudy yellow specimen, and the dull brown female, display distinctively different coloration. Bright, colorful wings on a moth are generally a signal that the species is active during the day, unlike the majority of its nocturnal relatives. Although it has no sting of its own, the wasp-mimicking moth's physical imitation of a more feared insect offers it a good deal of protection from predators.**

Metamorphosis is the stage-to-stage change that most species of insects undergo in developing from egg to adult. Moths and butterflies, like this monarch, pass through complete metamorphosis, which involves four distinctly different stages. This series of photos captures three of those stages. The caterpillar first affixes itself to a twig with a tiny "button" of silk. Next, the caterpillar undulates to split its skin and move it off its body, revealing the underlying soft green matter. In about an hour that green blob will harden, and the insect will be in its chrysalis stage.

In 11 to 13 days, the outer shell of the chrysalis will become clear, signaling that in less than a day a new butterfly will emerge. When the butterfly is ready, it will squirm about inside its shell to break it open. The insect will cling to the empty chrysalis, pumping blood into its wings, which will stretch to full size in a few minutes. It will rest a bit longer to allow the wings to dry and then will be ready to fly.

Other ants are farmers rather than ranchers. Harvester ants *(Pogonomyrmex barbatus)* gather plant seeds when they are abundant and store them in their hive for use during leaner times of the year. Many writers from biblical times on have made reference to the industriousness of these ants.

Still other insects rely on hunting. The wheel bug *(Arilus cristatus)* is equipped with a hypodermic-like beak, with which it injects venom into its insect prey and then sucks out the other creature's internal juices. The familiar praying mantis *(Mantis religiosa)* moves methodically through its habitat until some smaller insect happens too close and is speedily snatched by those front legs that give this predator its name.

The female tarantula hawk *(Hemipepsis)* – the world's largest wasp – cruises the southern U.S. in search of tarantulas. But the large spiders will not become the wasp's meal. Instead, the wasp paralyzes the tarantula with a venomous bite or two, lays her eggs on it, and buries the body. When the wasp grubs hatch from those eggs, they feed on the tarantula.

Preceding page: **The gatekeeper moth is named for the fact that it is commonly found along hedges, which often include gate areas. Its dullish coloring is well adapted to life in this environment.** *This page, top to bottom:* **After mating in June or July, the female great spangled fritillary goes into hiding until August or September, when it emerges to lay its eggs. The meadow fritillary, the most abundant butterfly species of North American wetlands, flies quickly near the ground in a jerky pattern. The loss of large tracts of undisturbed native forests has had a severe impact on populations of the Diana throughout the eastern U.S.**

Many species of tropical butterflies are very brightly colored. Such brilliant appearance lends very little camouflage protection, but is crucial to the insect for identifying possible mates of the same species. *Opposite:* So important to its courtship and mating is its bright coloring that the male of the blue morpho butterfly will be attracted to a piece of bright blue material waved in the air.

A caterpillar of the lime swallowtail chews its way through the leaf of a citrus tree. *Below:* Located just behind the heads of these two banded swallowtail caterpillars, where the bands cross their bodies, are organs called the *osmeteriums*. When threatened, the caterpillar instinctively protrudes this organ, which releases an offensive odor.

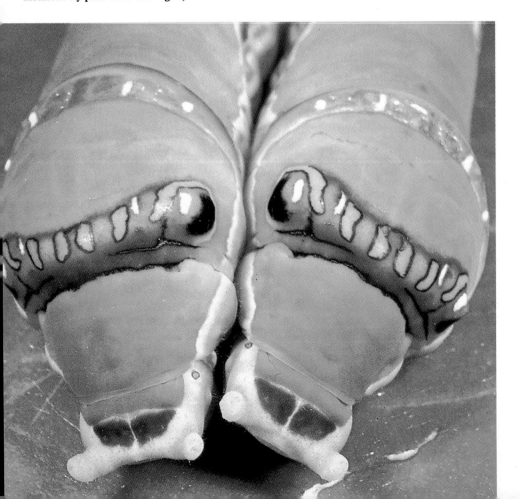

The tarantula hawk, like the other species included in these paragraphs, represents but a tiny portion of the great diversity that is the insect world. No one volume is equal to the task of cataloging and explaining it all. In fact, not all of it has yet been discovered. But hopefully this brief discussion will help dispel the creepy-crawly, pesky image of the insects and open a whole new world for you to explore, right at your feet.

The spicebush swallowtail protects itself from predators by mimicking the pipe-vine swallowtail, which predators generally avoid because of its foul flavor. *Below:* Also called the orange dog by frustrated citrus farmers, the giant swallowtail is generally regarded as an agricultural pest.

Although its migrations are somewhat shorter and much less renowned, the buckeye makes annual journeys north and south along the east coast of North America that are similar to those of the monarch. *Opposite:* The painted lady, also known as the cosmopolite, is the most widespread butterfly species on earth. Although absent from northern climates during late fall and winter, the species is found throughout North America, Europe, Asia, and Africa. *Overleaf:* The transparent wings of butterflies like this *Satyridae* are caused by reduced scaling across the insect's wings.

Index of Photography

TIB indicates The Image Bank